BOA
EDITIONS
LIMITED

The printing of this book was made possible, in part,
by generous donations from the Mary S. Mulligan Charitable Trust
and J. Christine Wilson and Mary K. Collins

MERCY

poems by

LUCILLE CLIFTON

■

american poets continuum series, no. 86

BOA Editions, Ltd.   ■   Rochester, NY   ■   2004

First Edition
04 05 06 07   7 6 5 4 3 2 1

Publications by BOA Editions, Ltd.—
a not-for-profit corporation under section 501 (c) (3)
of the United States Internal Revenue Code—
are made possible with the assistance of grants from
the Literature Program of the New York State Council on the Arts,
the Literature Program of the National Endowment for the Arts,
the Sonia Raiziss Giop Charitable Foundation,
the Lannan Foundation,
as well as from the Mary S. Mulligan Charitable Trust,
the County of Monroe, NY,
Ames-Amzalak Memorial Trust,
The CIRE Foundation,
and the Rochester Area Community Foundation.

See colophon on page 80 for special individual acknowledgments.

Cover Design: Geri McCormick
Cover Art: "Winter Evening on the Muck" by Richard C. Harrington
Interior Design and Composition: Richard Foerster
Manufacturing: McNaughton & Gunn
BOA Logo: Mirko

Library of Congress Cataloging-in-Publication Data

Clifton, Lucille, 1936–
  Mercy : poems / by Lucille Clifton.— 1st ed.
      p. cm. — (American poets continuum series ; v. 86)
  ISBN 1–929918–54–2 (hardcover : alk. paper); ISBN 1–929918–55–0 (pbk. :
alk. paper)
  I. Title. II. Series.

  PS3553.L45M47 2004
  811'.54—dc22   2004010396

NATIONAL
ENDOWMENT
FOR THE ARTS

BOA Editions, Ltd.
Thom Ward, Editor
David Oliveiri, Chair
A. Poulin, Jr., President & Founder (1938–1996)
260 East Avenue, Rochester, NY 14604
www.boaeditions.org

State of the Arts

NYSCA

contents

**the message from The Ones
(received in the late 70s)**

Always Rica   1961–2000
Always Chan   1962–2004

". . . the only mercy is memory"

last words

the gift

there was a woman who hit her head
and ever after she could see the sharp
wing of things   blues and greens
radiating from the body of her sister
her mother   her friends   when she felt

in her eyes the yellow sting
of her mothers dying   she trembled
but did not speak   her bent brain
stilled her tongue so that her life
became flash after flash of silence

bright as flame   she is gone now
her head knocked again against a door
that opened for her only
i saw her last in a plain box smiling
behind her sewn eyes there were hints
of purple and crimson and gold

■

out of body

(mama)

the words
they fade
i sift
toward other languages
you must listen
with your hands
with the twist ends
of your hair
that leaf
pick up
the sharp green stem
try to feel me feel you
i am saying I still love you
i am saying
i am trying to say
i am trying to say
from my mouth
but baby there is no
mouth

■

dying

i saw a small moon rise
from the breast of a woman
lying in a hospital hall
and I saw that the moon was me
and I saw that the punctured bag
of a woman body was me
and i saw you sad there in the lobby
waiting to visit and I wanted
to sing to you
go home
i am waiting for you there

∎

last words

(mama)

i am unforming
out of flesh

into the rubble
of the ground

there will be
new scars new tests

new "Mamas"
coming around

■

oh antic God
return to me
my mother in her thirties
leaned across the front porch
the huge pillow of her breasts
pressing against the rail
summoning me in for bed.

I am almost the dead woman's age times two.

I can barely recall her song
the scent of her hands
though her wild hair scratches my dreams
at night.   return to me, oh Lord of then
and now, my mother's calling,
her young voice humming my name.

■

april

bird and bird
over the thawing river
circling   parker
waving his horn
in the air above the osprey's
nest   my child
smiling her I know something
smile   their birthday
is coming   they are trying
to be forty   they will fail
they will fall
each from a different year
into the river   into the bay
into an ocean of marvelous things

■

after one year

she who was beautiful
entered Lake-Too-Soon without warning us
that it would storm in
our hearts forever   that it would
alter the landscape of our lives
and that at night we would
fold ourselves into
towels into blankets anything
trying to stop our eyes
from drowning themselves

■

sonku

his heart, they said, was
three times the regular size.
yes, i said, i know.

■

children

they are right, the poet mother
carries her wolf in her heart,
wailing at pain yet suckling it like
romulus and remus.   this now.
how will I forgive myself
for trying to bear the weight of this
and trying to bear the weight also
of writing the poem
about this?

■

stories

surely i am able to write poems
celebrating grass and how the blue
in the sky can flow green or red
and the waters lean against the
chesapeake shore like a familiar,
poems about nature and landscape
surely   but whenever i begin
"the trees wave their knotted branches
and . . ."   why
is there under that poem always
an other poem?

■

mulberry fields

they thought the field was wasting
and so they gathered the marker rocks and stones and
piled them into a barn   they say that the rocks were shaped
some of them scratched with triangles and other forms   they
must have been trying to invent some new language they say
the rocks went to build that wall there guarding the manor and
some few were used for the state house
crops refused to grow
i say the stones marked an old tongue and it was called eternity
and pointed toward the river   i say that after that collection
no pillow in the big house dreamed   i say that somewhere under
here moulders one called alice whose great grandson is old now
too and refuses to talk about slavery   i say that at the
masters table only one plate is set for supper   i say no seed
can flourish on this ground once planted then forsaken   wild
berries warm a field of bones
bloom how you must i say

■

the river between us

in the river that your father fished
my father was baptized.   it was
their hunger that defined them,

one, a man who knew he could
feed himself if it all came down,
the other a man who knew he needed help.

this is about more than color. it is
about how we learn to see ourselves.
it is about geography and memory.

it is about being poor people
in america.   it is about my father
and yours and you and me and
the river that is between us.

■

cancer

the first time the dreaded word
bangs against your eyes so that
you think you must have heard it but
what you know is that the room
is twisting crimson on its hinge
and all the other people there are dolls
watching from their dollhouse chairs

the second time you hear a swoosh as if
your heart has fallen down a well
and shivers in the water there
trying to not drown

the third time and you are so tired
so tired and you nod your head
and smile and walk away from
the angel uniforms the blood
machines and you enter the nearest
movie house and stand in the last aisle
staring at the screen with your living eyes

■

in the mirror

an only breast
leans against her chest wall
mourning   she is suspended
in a sob between t and e and a and r
and the gash ghost of her sister

t and e and a and r

it is pronounced like crying
it is pronounced like
being torn away
it is pronounced like trying to re
member the shape of an unsafe life

■

blood

here in this ordinary house
a girl is pressing a scarf
against her bleeding body
this is happening now

she will continue for over
thirty years emptying and
filling   sistering the moon
on its wild ride

men will march to games and wars
pursuing the bright red scarf
of courage   heroes every moon

some will die   while every moon
blood will enter this ordinary room
this ordinary girl will learn
to live with it

■

a story

for edgar

whose father is that
guarding the bedroom door
watching out for prowling
strangers for beasts and ogres
like in the childrens tale

not yours not mine

ours loomed there in the half
shadow of a daughters room
moaning a lullaby
in a wolfs voice

later
our mothers went mad and
our brothers killed themselves
and we began this storytelling life
wondering whose father that was
wondering how did we survive
to live not happily perhaps but

ever after

■

mercy

how grateful I was when he decided
not to replace his fingers with his thing
though he thought about it was going to
but mumbled "maybe I shouldn't do that"
and didn't do that and I was so
grateful then and now grateful
how sick   i am   how mad

■

here rests

my sister Josephine
born july in '29
and dead these 15 years
who carried a book
on every stroll.

when daddy was dying
she left the streets
and moved back home
to tend him.

her pimp came too
her Diamond Dick
and they would take turns
reading

a bible aloud through the house.
when you poem this
and you will   she would say
remember the Book of Job.

happy birthday and hope
to you Josephine
one of the easts
most wanted.

may heaven be filled
with literate men
may they bed you
with respect.

■

after oz

midnight we slip into her room
and fill her pockets with stones
so that she is weighted down
so that storms cannot move her

she disappears for hours
then staggers back smelling of straw
of animal

perhaps we have lost her
perhaps home is no longer comfort
or comfort no longer home

evenings we sit awake in
our disenchanted kitchen
listening to the dog whine
to dorothy clicking her heels

■

the Phantom

in his purple mask
his purple body suit
lived with a wolf
called Devil

the village believed him
immortal
the-ghost-who-walks
though he was only a man

i would save up
to go watch him
in his cave of skulls
his penthouse in the city

he would fall in love
with a white girl
like all the heroes
and monsters did

i was a little brown girl

after the show I would
walk home wondering
what would he feel
if he saw me

what is the color of
his country
what is the color
of mine

■

Powell

"i am your worst nightmare"
                    — black man to white

this is that dream I wake from
crying, then clutch my sleeping wife
and rock her until i fall again
onto a battlefield.   there,
they surround me, nations of darkness
speaking a language i cannot understand
and i suspect that something about
my life they know and hate and i hate them
for knowing it so well.   my son,
i think about my son, my golden daughter,
and as they surround me, nearer, nearer,
i reach to pick up anything,
a tool, a stick, a weapon and
something begins to die.   this
is that dream.

(powell was one of the officers
who beat rodney king.)

■

walking the blind dog

for wsm

        then he walks the blind dog muku
named for the dark of the moon
out to the park where she can smell
the other dogs and hear their
yips their puppy dreams

her one remaining eye is star lit
though it has no sight and
in its bright blue crater
is a vision of the world

old travelers who feel the way from here
to there and back again
who follow through the deep
grass the ruff of breeze
rustling her black coat   his white hair

both of them
poets
trusting the blind road home

■

hands

the snips of finger
fell from the sterile bowl
into my mind and after that
whatever i was taught they would
point toward a different learning
which i followed

i could no more ignore
the totems of my tribe
than i could close my eyes
against the light flaring
behind what has been called
the world

look   hold these regulated hands
against the sky
see how they were born to more
than bone   see how their shadow
steadies what i remain   whole
alive   twelvefingered

■

wind on the st. marys river

january 2002

it is the elders trying to return
sensing the coast is near and they
will soon be home again

they have walked under two oceans
and too many seas
the nap of their silver hair whipping
as the wind sings out to them
this way   this way

and they come rising steadily not
swimming exactly toward shore
toward redemption
but the wind dies down

and they sigh and still and descend
while we watch from our porches
not remembering their names not calling out
Jeremiah   Fanny Lou   Geronimo   but only

white caps on the water   look white caps

■

the tale the shepherds tell the sheep

that some will rise
above shorn clouds of fleece
and some will feel their bodies break
but most will pass through this
into sweet clover
where all   all will be sheltered safe
until the holy shearing
don't think about the days to come
sweet meat
think of my arms
trust me

■

stop

what you are doing
stop
what you are not doing
stop
what you are seeing
stop
what you are not seeing
stop
what you are hearing
stop
what you are not hearing
stop
what you are believing
stop
what you are not believing

in the green hills
of hemingway
nkosi has died
again
and again
and again

stop

—for Nkosi Johnson
2/4/89–6/1/01

■

september song
a poem in 7 days

1   tuesday 9/11/01

thunder and lightning and our world
is another place   no day
will ever be the same   no blood
untouched

they know this storm in otherwheres
israel   ireland   palestine
but God has blessed America
we sing

and God has blessed America
to learn that no one is exempt
the world is one   all fear

is one   all life   all death
all one

2 wednesday 9/12/01

this is not the time
i think
to note the terrorist
inside
who threw the brick
into the mosque
this is not the time
to note
the ones who cursed
Gods other name
the ones who threatened
they would fill the streets
with arab children's blood
and this is not the time
i think
to ask who is allowed to be
american   America
all of us gathered under one flag
praying together safely
warmed by the single love
of the many tongued God

3   thursday 9/13/01

the firemen
ascend
like jacobs ladder
into the mouth of
history

4   friday 9/14/01

some of us know
we have never felt safe

all of us   americans
weeping

as some of us have wept
before

is it treason to remember

what have we done
to deserve such villainy

nothing we reassure ourselves
nothing

5   saturday 9/15/01

i know a man who perished for his faith.
others called him infidel, chased him down
and beat him like a dog.   after he died
the world was filled with miracles.
people forgot he was a jew and loved him.
who can know what is intended?   who can understand
the gods?

6   sunday morning 9/16/01

for bailey

the st. marys river flows
as if nothing has happened

i watch it with my coffee
afraid and sad as are we all

so many ones to hate and i
cursed with long memory

cursed with the desire to understand
have never been good at hating

now this new granddaughter
born into a violent world

as if nothing has happened

and i am consumed with love
for all of it

the everydayness of bravery
of hate of fear of tragedy

of death and birth and hope
true as this river

and especially with love
bailey fredrica clifton goin

for you

7   **monday sundown 9/17/01**

Rosh Hashanah

i bear witness to no thing
more human than hate

i bear witness to no thing
more human than love

apples and honey
apples and honey

what is not lost
is paradise

■

the message from The Ones

(received in the late 70s)

beginning of message

your mother sends you this

you have a teapot
others have teapots
if you abuse them
they will break

you have a gift
others have gifts
if you abuse them

you understand

she advises you
you are special to her
she advises you
we are not she

■

come to here
each morning
for a word

we will bring
logos
with us
to this table
this chair

meet us here
each morning   yes

why you
why not

■

you
are not chosen

any stone
can sing

we come
to languages
not lives

your tongue
is useful
not unique

■

we are ones
who have not rolled
selves into bone and flesh

call us the ones

we will call you
one eye
field of feeling
singing ear
quick hand

we will make use
of these

■

in the saying of
you
we will sometime
be general
and sometime
particular

in the saying of we
we are we

■

we are here
between the lines

you reach through us
to raise your morning cup

you have assigned us countries
of the dead
but we are neither dead
nor emigrant

we are just here
where you are

■

why should we wander bone yards
draped in linen

flesh is the coat we unfasten
and throw off

what need to linger among stones
and monuments

we have risen away from all that
wrapped in understanding

■

some of you have been blessed
or cursed
to see beyond yourselves

into the scattered wrongful dead
into the disappeared
the despised

none of you has seen
everything
none of you has said
everything

what you have not noticed
we have noticed
what you have ignored
we have not

■

you come to teach
and to learn

you do not know
anothers lesson

pay attention to
what sits inside yourself
and watches you

you may sometime discover
which when
which which

■

in the geometry
of knowing
we have no new thing
to tell
only the same old
almanac
january
love one another
february
whatever you sow
you will reap

∎

we
who have not been
human
have not learned
to love it
more

human is neither
wiser
nor more blessed

it is not wise
to count oneself
the only servant
of ones lord

it is not wise
to count oneself
the favorite servant
of ones lord

■

god
is
love

no

god
is love
is light
is god

no

place here
the name
you give
to god
is love
is light
is
here the name
you give
to

yes

■

the angels have no wings
they come to you wearing
their own clothes

they have learned to love you
and will keep coming

unless you insist on wings

■

you who feel yourself
drowning in the bodys need
what can you know clearly
of fleshlessness

there is no hunger here
we come to you directly
without touching

you who lie awake
holding your mouth open
receive us as best you can
and we enter you

as we must
tongueless
as best we can

■

you wish to speak of
black and white
no
you wish to hear of
black and white

have we not talked of human

every human comes
to every color
some remember
some do not

■

you are not
your brothers keeper
you are
your brother

the one
hiding in the bush
is you

the one
lying on the grate
is you

the mad one in the cage
or at the podium
is you

the king is you
the kike is you
the honky is you
the nigger is you
the bitch is you
the beauty is you
the friend is you
the enemy   oh

others have come
to say this
it is not
metaphor

you are not
your sisters keeper
you are
your sister   yes

■

the universe requires the worlds
to be
each leaf is veined from the mother/ father
each heart is veined from the mother/ father
each leaf each heart has a place
irreplaceable
each is required to be

■

you have placed yourselves
in peril
not by your superior sword
but by your insignificant
quarrels with life

no   by your quarrels with
insignificant life   yes

there are some languages
some fields some sky
the lord of language field and sky
is lonely for

they have been worlds
they will be worlds again

your world is in grave danger

■

whether in spirit
or out of spirit
we don't know

only that balance
is the law

balance
or be balanced

whether in body
or out of body
we don't know

■

the air
you have polluted
you will breathe

the waters
you have poisoned
you will drink

when you come again
and you will come again

the air
you have polluted
you will breathe

the waters
you have poisoned
you will drink

∎

the patience
of the universe
is not without
an end

so might it
slowly
turn its back

so might it
slowly
walk away

leaving you alone
in the world you leave
your children

■

what has been made
can be unmade

saints have begun to enter
wearing breasts
hoping for children
nursed toward wholeness
holiness

it is perhaps
a final chance

not the end of the world
of a world

■

there is a star
more distant
than eden
something there
is even now
preparing

■

end of message

acknowledgments

Grateful acknowledgment is made to the editors of the following journals, in which some of these poems first appeared: *Callaloo, Kestrel, Lyric,* and *Runes.* Thanks also to National Public Radio, which aired Ms. Clifton reading her sequence "september song: a poem in 7 days."

■

about the author

Lucille Clifton is the author of eleven books of poetry, one prose collection and nineteen books for children. Her collection, *Blessing the Boats: New and Selected Poems 1988–2000* received the National Book Award for Poetry. Other honors include an Emmy Award from the American Academy of Television Arts & Sciences, two fellowships from the National Endowment for the Arts, the Shelley Memorial Prize, the Charity Randall Citation, and a Lannan Literary Award. In 1996, she was a National Book Award Finalist for *The Terrible Stories* and was the only poet ever to have two books (*next: new poems* and *good woman: poems and a memoir 1969–1980*) chosen as finalists for the Pulitzer Prize in the same year. Appointed a Chancellor of The Academy of American Poets in 1999 and elected a Fellow in Literature of The American Academy of Arts and Sciences, Clifton currently resides in Columbia, Maryland, where she is a Distinguished Professor of Humanities and holds the Hilda C. Landers Chair in the Liberal Arts at St. Mary's College.

■

BOA EDITIONS, LTD.: AMERICAN POETS CONTINUUM SERIES

colophon

Mercy, poems by Lucille Clifton, was set in Optima fonts
by Richard Foerster, York Beach, Maine.
The cover was designed by Geri McCormick, Rochester, New York.
Manufacturing by McNaughton & Gunn, Ann Arbor, Michigan.

■

The publication of this book was made possible,
in part, by the special support of the following individuals:

Nelson Blish
Dr. & Mrs. Gary H. Conners
Carole Cooper & Howard Haims
Burch & Louise Craig
Ronald & Susan Dow
Suzanne & Peter Durant
Suressa Forbes
Dr. Henry & Beverly French
Judy & Dane Gordon
Marge & Don Grinols
Kip & Deb Hale
Peter & Robin Hursh ■ Robert & Willy Hursh
Linda Kaplan
Archie & Pat Kutz
Lester & Deborah Lennon
Rosemary & Lew Lloyd
John & Lillian Maguire
David & Marianne Oliveiri
Boo Poulin
Deborah Ronnen
Deborah D. Ruth
Jane Schuster ■ Robert Shea
Allen & Suzy Spencer
Celia Jane Stuart-Powles
George Wallace
Ellen P. Wallack
Thomas R. Ward
Pat & Michael Wilder
Glenn & Helen William
Geraldine Zetzel